DANGEROUS

Extreme
Exploration

JOHN MALAM

FRANKLIN WATTS
LONDON • SYDNEY

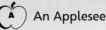 An Appleseed Editions book

First published in 2008 by Franklin Watts

Paperback edition 2009

Franklin Watts
338 Euston Road, London NW1 3BH

Franklin Watts Australia
Hachette Children's Books
Level 17/207 Kent St, Sydney, NSW 2000

© 2008 Appleseed Editions

Appleseed Editions Ltd
Well House, Friars Hill, Guestling, East Sussex TN35 4ET

Created by Q2A Media
Series Editor: Jean Coppendale; Book Editor: Paul Manning
Senior Art Designers: Ashita Murgai, Nishant Mudgal
Designer: Shilpi Sarkar; Picture Researcher: Lalit Dalal
Line Artists: Amit Tayal, Sibi N.D
Illustrators: Aadil Ahmed Siddiqui, Mahender Kumar, Sanyogita Lal

ISBN 978 0 7496 9277 3

Dewey classification: 910.92

All words in **bold** can be found in the glossary on page 30.

Website information is correct at time of going to press. However, the publishers cannot
accept liability for any information or links found on third-party websites.

A CIP catalogue for this book is available from the British Library.

Picture credits
t=top b=bottom c=centre l=left r=right m=middle
Cover: Q2A Media
Hirlesteanu Constantin-Ciprian: 4-5 (background), Science Photo Library/ Photolibrary: 6t,
Historical Picture Archive/ Corbis: 8t, The Mariners Museum: 8b, FCIT: 9, Melking/ Dreamstime.com: 10l,
Sheila Terry/ Science Photo Library/ Photolibrary: 11t, James Steidl: 11b, Royal Geographical Society: 13,
Corbis: 14, Royal Geographical Society: 15t, 15b, Science Photo Library/ Photolibrary: 16, Gary Parker/
Science Photo Library/ Photolibrary: 17t, Mary Evans Picture Library/ Photolibrary: 17b, Hulton-Deutsch
Collection/ Corbis: 20t, Cambridge University Library/ Royal Commonwealth Society Library: 20b,
Frank Hurley/ www.shackleton-endurance.com: 23t, Marek CECH: 25tl, The Lordprice Collection: 25tr,
Hulton Archive/ Getty Images: 26t, NASA: 26b, 27, 28, 29.

Printed in China

Franklin Watts is a division of Hachette Children's Books,
an Hachette UK company.
www.hachette.co.uk

Contents

THE CALL OF THE UNKNOWN

*In ancient times many people were scared to travel beyond the **horizon**. Some thought it was the very edge of the world. Others believed there were monsters on the other side. Luckily there were always some who were willing to 'go the extra mile', risking their lives to discover new lands and far-off places.*

The voyage of Pytheas

Long ago, an ancient Greek explorer called Pytheas made history when he ventured into the unknown. His ship left Massilia (now Marseilles), sailed out of the Mediterranean Sea and headed for the Atlantic. He travelled along the coasts of France and Spain, and then to Britain.

On his voyage Pytheas saw sights and landscapes that were undreamed of in the Mediterranean lands from which he came

Land of the midnight sun

Not only did Pytheas become the first known person to sail around Britain, but he sailed as far north as he could go.

Pytheas saw an ocean covered in ice, and a strange land where it was daylight most of the time, which he named 'Thule'. Today, we think that Pytheas had reached Iceland and the Arctic Ocean. It is amazing to think that his journey took place 2,300 years ago. He travelled about 12,800 km, making it one of the longest sea journeys of ancient times.

Modern explorers

Since the time of Pytheas, explorers have continued to make difficult and dangerous journeys to faraway places. Although travel is much less dangerous today, the exploits of explorers such as Ernest Shackleton (see page 21) and Neil Armstrong (see page 26) prove that there are still plenty of exciting adventures to be had and discoveries to be made.

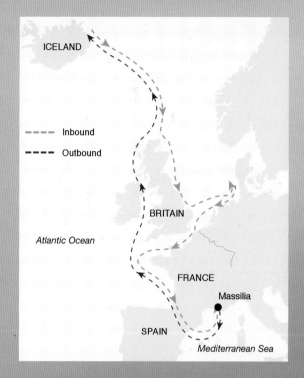

The possible route of Pytheas' voyage from the Mediterranean to Iceland and the Arctic Ocean

'In Thule, the earth and sea and everything else are held in suspense, through which one can neither walk nor sail.'

Pytheas, describing the frozen Arctic Ocean

FIRST AROUND THE WORLD

Ferdinand Magellan and the voyage of the Victoria

In September 1522 a party of sailors returned to Spain with an amazing story to tell. Their ship, the Victoria, was the only survivor of a fleet of five. They had been the first to sail around the world – but they had returned without their brave captain, Ferdinand Magellan.

A journey of discovery

Three years earlier, Magellan's fleet had set out to discover a new route to the Spice Islands, a rich source of cloves, nutmeg and pepper, which were worth their weight in gold at the time.

The islands were far away, and could only be reached by a long and dangerous voyage around Africa and across the Indian Ocean. Magellan believed he could find a new route to the Spice Islands for Spain, not by sailing east like everyone else, but by heading west. Magellan was determined to take the risk - and ended up finding something that no one had expected.

Ferdinand Magellan

Ferdinand Magellan (1480–1521) was the first explorer to sail westward from Europe to Asia and across the Pacific. Born in Portugal, he served his country well, but after an argument with the king, he swapped sides and went to work for his country's rival, Spain.

In the sixteenth century, spices were highly valuable and were used for flavouring foods and in medicines and cosmetics. Spain and Portugal were fierce rivals for control of the spice trade

'On Monday morning,
August 10, St Lawrence's Day,
in the year 1519, the fleet,
having been supplied with
all the things necessary for
the sea and men of every sort
(our number was two
hundred and thirty-seven),
we made ready to leave.'
Antonio Pigafetta (c.1491–c.1534),
a traveller with Magellan, describing
the start of the voyage

Ferdinand Magellan studies the route
his fleet of ships will take on their round-
the-world voyage

Trouble ahead

Magellan did not want to frighten his men, so he did not tell them about the route he planned to take - or how long the voyage might be.

After sailing down the coast of West Africa, the little fleet crossed the Atlantic to South America. Failing to find a route across the continent, they headed south and into uncharted waters. Winter was approaching, so Magellan found a safe place to land. For the next five months he tried to keep his men busy - but there was trouble ahead.

MUTINY!

With food in short supply, Magellan put the men on **rations**. Soon he was facing a **mutiny**. He had to take control - fast. Some men had stayed on his side, and he sent them to round up the troublemakers. One mutineer was hacked to bits, another was executed. A third was put ashore and left. Magellan had shown he was in charge, whether his men liked it or not.

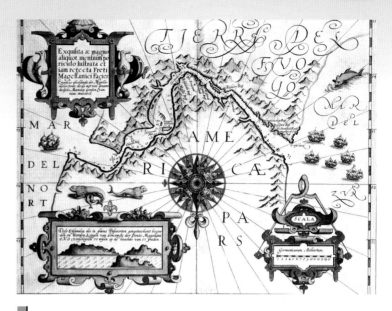

An early map showing the narrow sea route between Chile and Terra del Fuego in South America, now known as the Magellan Strait

The Magellan Strait

On 21 October 1520, the ships entered a narrow **strait** of water around the tip of South America. It was a difficult route, with wild seas, high winds and constant danger from rocks, but eventually, after almost forty days, the strait which now bears Magellan's name was behind them. The *Victoria* and her sister ships had entered an unknown ocean, which Magellan named the Pacific, meaning 'peaceful'.

As Magellan leads the way in a small boat, his ships sail through the narrow, rocky strait at the tip of South America

The death of Magellan

Despite the hardships of the voyage, which included **malnutrition** and **malaria**, Magellan pressed on, sailing westward across the Pacific. After a hundred days land was sighted. At last, the men had fresh food to eat. But at Mactan, an island in the Philippines, disaster struck. In a fierce fight with hostile islanders Magellan was killed. Despite his death, the surviving crew members refused to give up their captain's quest. In November 1521 they finally reached the Spice Islands.

Caught in a dispute between rival tribes of islanders, Magellan meets his death on the shores of Mactan in the Philippines

Magellan's voyage

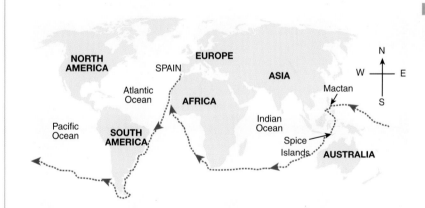

Magellan's round-the-world voyage took three years, from 1519 to 1522. The aim was to find a new route to the Spice Islands, by sailing west instead of east. Of the five ships that left Spain, only the Victoria returned home. The others were lost on the voyage

20 September 1519	The fleet leaves Spain and begins to cross the Atlantic Ocean
March 1520	Spends winter at Puerto San Julian, southern Argentina
September 1520	Mutiny breaks out
21 October 1520	Begins to round the tip of South America, leaving the Atlantic and entering the Pacific Ocean
6 March 1521	First **landfall** after 100 days out of sight of land
27 April 1521	Magellan killed on the island of Mactan, Philippines
6 September 1522	The *Victoria* reaches Spain

JOURNEY'S END

By the time the *Victoria* finally reached home, there were just 18 men on board out of the original crew of 237 - but the ship's valuable cargo of spice more than paid for the expedition.

Ferdinand Magellan had indeed found a new route to the Spice Islands, but more than that, he had proved the world was round, not flat, and far bigger than most people imagined. In the process he had lost his life, but his name is for ever linked with these great discoveries.

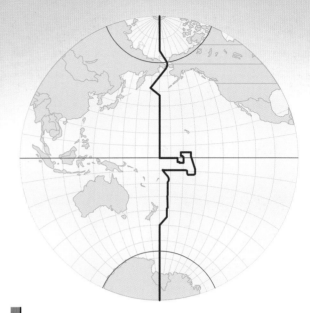

On their return, the crew of the Victoria *were puzzled to find they had arrived home a day earlier than they thought. In fact, they had crossed the **International Date Line** (shown in red above) where the date changes by a day – forwards or backwards depending on whether you are travelling east or west*

In the sixteenth century, the hourglass was one of the only reliable ways of telling the time at sea. Each of Magellan's ships had 18 hourglasses on board which had to be 'turned' by a special member of the crew

Surviving a long sea voyage

Describing life on board the *Victoria*, Antonio Pigafetta wrote: 'We ate biscuit, which was no longer biscuit, but powder of biscuits swarming with worms, and drank yellow water that had been **putrid** for many days.'

Could you have survived the voyage? Which would have been the worst part for you?

- Fear of the unknown
- Storms and gales
- Cramped quarters
- Seasickness
- Terrible food
- Feeling homesick
- Rats!

IN SEARCH OF AFRICA
The story of David Livingstone

As David Livingstone explored central Africa, he had no idea what he would find along the course of the Zambezi River. It was 1855, and Livingstone was searching for trade routes that would bring Christianity to Africa and end the slave trade.

Defeating slavery

As a **missionary**, Livingstone had worked in central Africa for many years and had seen the horrors of the slave trade (see below) at first hand. He felt sure that if traders and missionaries could travel to the centre of Africa along the river system, then slavery could be defeated. And so, in 1854, he began his search to find a river route into the heart of Africa.

David Livingstone (1813–73) was born in Blantyre, Scotland, the son of a Sunday school teacher. A missionary and explorer, Livingstone was also a pioneer of trade in Africa. His motto, inscribed on his statue at the foot of the Victoria Falls, is 'Christianity, Commerce and Civilization'

The African slave trade

Between 1450 and 1850, millions of African men, women and children were uprooted from their homes and sold into slavery. Slaves were seen as the 'property' of their masters, forced to work without pay or reward and brutally treated. By Livingstone's time, the European slave trade was largely at an end, but Arab and African slave-traders still brought misery to many parts of North and East Africa.

Livingstone gazes in awe at the world's largest waterfall. He later described the Victoria Falls as 'the most wonderful sight' he had witnessed in all his travels in Africa

THE SMOKE THAT THUNDERS

Livingstone's search took him back and forth across central Africa, from Angola in the west to Mozambique in the east. Despite disease and danger, he never gave up.

On 17 November 1855, Livingstone reached a place known by Africans as Mosi-oa-Tunya or 'the smoke that thunders'. Before him was a sight never before seen by a European. Shrouded in mist and vapour, the Zambezi River seemed to disappear, falling over a cliff as a great sheet of water. It was the world's largest waterfall. Livingstone named it Victoria Falls in honour of Victoria, the queen of England.

It took 18 months for Livingstone to complete his journey, covering 6,900 km. In so doing he became the first European to cross Africa from coast to coast.

The Zambezi expedition, 1858

Back in England, Livingstone found himself a national hero. He had no trouble raising money for a new expedition. This time he planned to explore the Zambezi in detail, and build a missionary station along its route.

From the start things went wrong. The party's paddle-boat turned out to be a bad choice for the Zambezi **rapids**. Quarrels broke out, and even though a mission station was built, it was abandoned when the missionaries died. Livingstone's wife Mary, who joined him in Africa in 1862, died of fever. After six years, Livingstone returned to Britain, but the public had lost interest in his work and he was no longer treated as a celebrity.

*'I peered down into a large rent which had been made from bank to bank of the broad Zambezi, and saw that a stream of a thousand yards broad leaped down a hundred feet, and then became suddenly compressed into a space of fifteen or twenty yards. The entire falls are simply a crack made in the hard **basaltic** rock ... the most wonderful sight I had witnessed in Africa.'*

David Livingstone,
Missionary Travels and Researches in South Africa (1857)

Attacked by a hippo

Livingstone's travels in Africa were often hard and dangerous. Attacks by lions and other wild animals were not unusual. This picture shows his canoe being capsized by an angry hippopotamus.

'DR LIVINGSTONE, I PRESUME?'

Despite the failure of the Zambezi expedition, David Livingstone was still the most famous explorer of his day, and he dreamed of one last mission. This time he wanted to find the source of the Nile, the greatest waterway in Africa. It was a mystery that had fascinated explorers for many years.

Livingstone and a team of 60 **porters** crossed East Africa to Lake Malawi and then on to Lake Tanganyika, where he was taken ill. Nothing was heard from him for three years. There were rumours that he was dead – but was he? In 1869, Henry Morton Stanley, an American journalist, was sent to Africa by his newspaper, the *New York Herald*. His orders were simple: 'Find Livingstone.'

Map of central Africa showing the routes travelled by Livingstone between the years 1851 and 1873

Stanley's meeting with Livingstone made headline news around the world. Stanley wrote: 'I walked deliberately to him, took off my hat, and said: "Dr Livingstone, I presume?" 'Yes," said he, with a kind smile, lifting his hat slightly'

Famous meeting

On 10 November 1871, Stanley 'found' the missing explorer in a village on the shore of Lake Tanganyika. It was one of the most famous meetings of all time. (In fact, Livingstone did not think of himself as being 'lost' – just resting while he recovered from illness.)

Stanley stayed with Livingstone, helping him explore the northern end of Lake Tanganyika, which they discovered was not the source of the Nile. Eventually, they parted company. Stanley went to England, and Livingstone stayed in Africa, where he died in 1873. His heart was buried there, but his body was buried in Westminster Abbey, London.

Livingstone the missionary

For some people, David Livingstone is a heroic figure who helped to bring civilization to the 'dark continent' of Africa. Others are not so sure: they argue that missionaries who impose their beliefs on 'primitive people' often do more harm than good.

What do YOU think? Write down three arguments for and against Livingstone the missionary.

David Livingstone: an explorer's life

1813	Born at Blantyre, near Glasgow, Scotland
1836	Studies medicine; plans to work as Christian missionary in Africa
1840	Becomes a doctor; joins London Missionary Society; sails to southern Africa to begin work as missionary
1849–51	Crosses Kalahari Desert
1853–6	Makes first west–east crossing of Africa by a European; first European to see Victoria Falls
1858–64	Attempts to navigate Zambezi River
1866–71	Searches for source of River Nile around Lake Tanganyika; falls ill and disappears
1871	Meets Henry Morton Stanley at Ujiji, in former Tanganyika
1873	Dies on shore of Lake Bangweulu.

Above: Livingstone's peaked cap and compass

UNCOMMON TRAVELLER
The story of Mary Kingsley

It was rare for a Victorian woman to become an explorer, but Mary Kingsley (1862–1900) was no ordinary woman. While others sat at home by the fireside, she travelled through unexplored parts of west and central Africa, living with local tribes and bringing back plants, insects and animals to study.

A taste for adventure

Mary Kingsley had first been inspired to visit Africa during a holiday in the Canary Islands. Back home in London, she began to make plans for a trip to the continent she had heard so much about.

It was August 1893 when her ship reached Sierra Leone. For the next few weeks Mary travelled up and down the West African coast and along the Congo River, trading with the local people and swapping tobacco for unusual fish and insects. It had been quite an adventure - and she had got the taste for exploring.

'I had got caught in a tornado in a dense forest. The massive mighty trees were waving like a wheatfield gale in England... The fierce rain came in a roar, tearing to shreds the leaves and blossoms and deluging everything.'
from Mary Kingsley, *Travels in West Africa* (1897)

Mary Kingsley was born in London, the daughter of a travel writer. She had little formal schooling, but she was allowed to read the books in her father's large library and loved to hear his tales of foreign countries

Return to Africa

On her second trip, Mary Kingsley knew what to expect and took equipment to help her collect **specimens** for the British Museum in London. She collected insects, shells, plants, 18 species of reptile and 65 species of fish, three of which were unknown to science.

Mary Kingsley travelled on foot through the jungles of Gabon, and down the Ogooué River in a canoe paddled by eight local people. It capsized many times, tipping her into the crocodile-infested river. She reached parts of West Africa where no European had been before, and she was one of the first 'outsiders' to meet and live alongside **cannibal** tribes such as the Fan people.

Dense jungle like this makes travel in West Africa difficult and dangerous, even today

Living with the Fan people

Mary Kingsley (seated, to the left of the flag) being ferried down the Ogooué River in what is now Gabon. When a crocodile attacked her canoe, Mary Kingsley fought it off with a paddle!

During her travels Mary Kingsley lived with local people, including the cannibal Fan tribe, and often ventured into dangerous areas alone. Very little seemed to shock or upset her.

She once found a human hand, three big toes, an eye, two ears and 'other portions of the human frame' in a tribesman's hut. She wrote: 'I later learnt that although the Fans will eat their fellow friendly tribesfolk, they like to keep a little something belonging to them as a **memento**.'

17

'MOUNTAIN OF THUNDER'

Returning by sea via the Cameroon coast, Mary Kingsley came upon an active volcano, known as 'Mongo-ma-Loba' ('Mountain of Thunder'). She was determined to climb it.

Rising up through the rainforest, Mount Cameroon, as it is known today, reaches a height of 4,095 m. Soaked through, her heavy skirts clinging to her legs, and splashed with mud, Mary Kingsley took six days to reach the summit. During the final part of the climb she had to scramble over barren, jagged volcanic rock and was caught in a violent hurricane. But she had made history as the first European to climb the mountain!

> *'I made my way up and after a desperate fight reached the cairn,* only, alas!, to find a hurricane raging and a fog in full possession, and not ten yards' view to be had in any direction... The rain lashes so fiercely I cannot turn my face to it and breathe, the wind is all I can do to stand up against.'*
>
> Mary Kingsley,
> Travels in West Africa *(1897)*

*Cairn: a pile of stones used to mark the highest point of a hill or mountain

Map of West Africa, showing the routes travelled by Mary Kingsley on her two expeditions. The exact route she followed between Matadi and Glass is not known

NIGERIA
Bonny Calabar
Mt Cameroon
4,095 m
Limbe
Malato
CAMEROON
Bight of Biafra
EQUATORIAL GUINEA
Libreville Glass
Ogooué River
GABON
CONGO
River Congo
Atlantic Ocean
Cabinda
ZAIRE
Matadi
ANGOLA

- - - - - - First Journey
- - - - - - Uncertain Route
- - - - - - Second Journey

Luanda

0   300 km
0   200 m

Pushing on through wind and rain, Mary Kingsley clambers upwards towards the 'Great peak of Cameroons'. The route she followed had never been attempted before by a European

'Courageous adventures'

Back in Britain, newspapers wrote about Mary Kingsley's 'surprising and courageous adventures', and she gave talks all over the country. She wrote books about her travels, describing the places, people and animals she had seen. To most people, Africa was a mysterious faraway place, and she hoped her books would give them a better understanding of the land she loved. She could not wait to return for a third visit. But it was not to be.

A NURSE IN THE BOER WAR

Mary Kingsley never did return to West Africa. Instead, in March 1900 she sailed to South Africa, where British soldiers were fighting in the Boer War. She planned to work there as a nurse, caring for the sick and injured.

Within days of arriving she was sent to work in a hospital for injured prisoners of war. It was a dirty and dangerous place, where a terrible disease called **typhoid** was killing the patients. It was not long before Mary Kingsley herself caught the disease and died. She was just 37 years old.

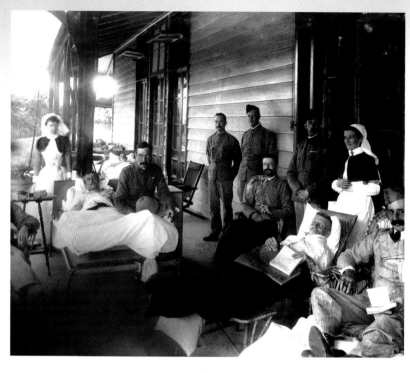

Nurses and patients at a hospital for soldiers wounded in the Boer War

Mary Kingsley: a traveller's life

1862	Born in London
1892	Visits the Canary Islands, off the coast of West Africa
1893	First visit to West Africa
1894–5	Second visit to West Africa. Climbs Mount Cameroon
1900	Dies in South Africa.

Could YOU have survived the dangers and discomforts faced by Mary Kingsley as she travelled through West Africa? Here are just a few of them:

- Bites and stings
- Violent storms and terrible weather
- Attacks by crocodiles and other wild animals
- Long journeys on foot through dense jungle
- Threat of attack by fierce cannibal tribes

TO THE ENDS OF THE EARTH
Ernest Shackleton, polar explorer

The legendary polar explorer Ernest Shackleton (1874–1922) is best remembered for the Endurance expedition, one of the greatest real-life adventure stories of all time. Crushed, trapped and choked by snow and ice, Shackleton and his men became castaways on Antarctica – the world's frozen continent.

Shackleton was no stranger to Antarctica and he knew what he was letting himself in for - or so he thought. His plan was to cross the icy continent on foot, a distance of 2,900 km over the toughest terrain on the planet. Shackleton's ship, the *Endurance,* set sail from England in August 1914 with a crew of 27. By December it had reached the Weddell Sea. And that is when the trouble began.

Ernest Shackleton, whose expedition to Antarctica turned into a desperate struggle for survival

South Georgia

Elephant Island

Lifeboats launched
9 April 1916

Weddell Sea

Endurance sank
21 November 1915

Abandoned ship
27 October 1915

Endurance trapped in ice
18 January 1915

ANTARCTICA

The route taken by Shackleton and his men during their epic journey across the Antarctic

TRAPPED IN THE ICE

The Weddell Sea was blocked with ice, and the *Endurance* was forced to stop. As the ice closed in, the ship became trapped and began to drift helplessly between the giant **floes**.

For nine months the crew remained on board the stricken ship, but when the pressure of the ice began to crack open the wooden hull, Shackleton had no choice but to abandon ship. From then on, it was a desperate fight for survival.

Shackleton and his crew salvage supplies from the stricken ship and prepare for their gruelling ordeal on the shifting ice floes of the Weddell Sea

'The ice is rafting up to a height of 10 or 15 feet in places... The noise resembles the roar of heaving, distant **surf**. Standing on the stirring ice, one can imagine it is disturbed by the breathing and tossing of a mighty giant below.'

from *South* (1919), Shackleton's account of the *Endurance* expedition

Ocean camp

In the freezing cold, the men struggled to salvage lifeboats and supplies from the wrecked ship. They set up a camp on the shifting ice, drifting with it as it inched its way over the Weddell Sea. Weeks turned into months. The *Endurance* gave in to the ice and sank. The stranded men feared for their lives. But Shackleton was made of strong stuff: he had no intention of being beaten by the extreme conditions.

As the camp drifted towards the sea, the ice thinned and cracked. It was time to take to the lifeboats. After a 160 km voyage through crumbling ice, Shackleton and his men reached the barren shore of Elephant Island - the first time in sixteen months they had set foot on solid ground.

Above: the Endurance, *frozen fast in the Weddell Sea. Shackleton wrote:* 'Though we have been compelled to abandon the ship … we are alive and well, and we have stores and equipment for the task that lies before us'

The camp on Elephant Island

Elephant Island, off the coast of Antarctica, had no natural shelter, and Shackleton and his men had to construct a makeshift shack from their remaining two lifeboats *(below right)*. **Blubber** lamps were used for lighting.

Food was scarce and the crew, many of whom were already ill and frostbitten, were close to starvation.

They hunted for penguins and seals, neither of which were plentiful during the autumn and winter months.

Marooned on Elephant Island, Shackleton's men lived together inside the tiny hut (right) for four and half months

23

TO HELL AND BACK

On Elephant Island the plight of Shackleton and his crew was desperate. It was obvious there was no chance of rescue from this hostile place. There was only one thing to do - make for South Georgia Island, 1,400 km away.

Survival against the odds

Shackleton picked five men to go with him, leaving the rest on Elephant Island. For two weeks their lifeboat, the *James Caird*, battled through stormy seas until at last they reached South Georgia - but on the wrong side. Tired and hungry, Shackleton and two out of the five men **trekked** over 240 km of icy cliffs and glaciers before finally reaching the island's whaling station, the world's southernmost outpost. They were safe at last.

Launching the James Caird *from the shore of Elephant Island, 24 April 1916. In one of the most incredible feats in the history of sailing and navigation, Shackleton and his five-man crew survived their 1,400 km voyage in an open boat, arriving at South Georgia almost two weeks later*

The barren Elephant Island where Shackleton's men survived four and half months of bitter cold and near-starvation

'*All night long we lay in the open, freezing sea ... four degrees below zero and a film of ice formed on the surface of the sea. When we were not on watch, we lay in each other's arms for warmth... Occasionally from an almost clear sky came snow showers, falling silently on the sea and laying a thin* **shroud** *of white over our bodies and our boats.*'

from Ernest Shackleton, South *(1919)*

Rescued!

Throughout the *Endurance* expedition, Shackleton had been determined to bring every member of the expedition back home safely. Now at last he was able to organize the rescue of the remaining members of his party.

From the whaling station at South Georgia, a ship was sent to pick up the three men who had been left on the other side of the island. Meanwhile, in a borrowed Chilean tugboat, the *Yelcho*, Shackleton finally broke through the ice surrounding Elephant Island to rescue all the men who had set out on the original expedition. Against the odds, every single member of his crew returned to England alive.

Perils of the Antarctic

Shackleton's concern for the safety of his men was one of the qualities that made him a great explorer and expedition leader.

What other qualities do you think you would need to lead an expedition to the South Pole? Here are few to start you off:

- Practical skills, including navigation and seamanship
- Resourcefulness
- Ability to make difficult decisions
- Physical courage, strength and stamina
- Mental toughness

Shackleton: an explorer's life

1874	Born in Kilkee, Ireland
1901–3	Travels to Antarctica with the National Antarctic Expedition
1907–9	Leads the British Antarctic Expedition
1914–17	Leads the Imperial Trans-Antarctic Expedition; loses his ship, the *Endurance*; survives extreme conditions before reaching safety
1922	Dies on South Georgia

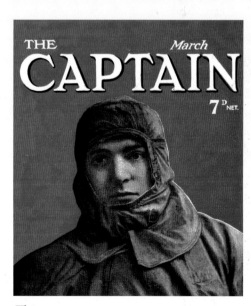

Ernest Shackleton, pictured on the front cover of the popular English magazine The Captain *in 1917*

MAN ON THE MOON
Neil Armstrong and the Apollo 11 landing

*On 20 July 1969 the dream of **lunar** exploration became reality when Neil Armstrong became the first person to set foot on the surface of the moon.*

The 'space race'

In the 1950s and 1960s, the world's two greatest powers, the USA and the **Soviet Union**, had tried to outdo each other with a series of space missions. The Soviet Union took the lead by launching the first **satellite**, by taking the first photographs of the far side of the moon and by putting the first person in space. But the ultimate goal was still there for the taking – to be the first nation to put a man on the moon.

*Above: In April 1961 Soviet **cosmonaut** Yuri Gagarin became the first person in space and the first to orbit the earth*
Below: The lunar module of the US Apollo 11, with the surface of the moon in the background

'I believe that this nation should commit itself to achieving the goal, before this decade is out, of landing a man on the moon and returning him safely to earth.'

US President John F Kennedy,
25 May 1961

The Apollo space programme

Throughout the 1960s, the American space agency NASA worked on a series of space missions. Bigger and more powerful rockets were tested, and more and more was learned about spaceflight. By 1967 the Apollo space programme was ready, but when three astronauts died at the very start, the mission to land men on the moon was nearly abandoned.

Each Apollo spacecraft was mounted on a Saturn 5 rocket, which had enough power to blast off into space. Apollo had three sections: the command module housed the crew; the lunar module would land on the moon, and the service module supplied Apollo with oxygen, water and fuel.

'We have lift-off!'

The moment the whole world had been waiting for came on 16 July 1969, when Apollo 11 lifted off from the Kennedy Space Center, Florida. On board were Neil A Armstrong, Edwin E 'Buzz' Aldrin, and Michael Collins.

After three days the tiny spacecraft entered the moon's **orbit**, circling it fourteen times. Then the time came for 'Eagle', the lunar module, to separate from the command module and head for the moon's surface. Inside were Neil Armstrong and 'Buzz' Aldrin. Michael Collins remained in the orbiting command module.

The Saturn 5 launch rocket carrying Apollo 11 blasts into space on 16 July 1969

Service module

Command module

Lunar module

Third stage rocket

Second stage rocket

First stage rocket

'THE EAGLE HAS LANDED'

As Armstrong approached the area chosen for the moon landing, he could see it was littered with rocks. Acting quickly, he diverted the lunar module to a smoother place. When the Eagle touched down, it had fuel left for just 45 seconds.

For the next few hours Armstrong and Aldrin prepared for man's first steps on the moon. A television camera on the outside of the Eagle sent fuzzy black-and-white pictures back to a waiting world of the historic moment when Neil Armstrong climbed down the ladder of the Eagle. As he took his first step on the moon's grey surface, he said the famous words: 'That's one small step for man, one giant leap for mankind.'

'We're going to the moon because it's in the nature of the human being to face challenges. It's by the nature of his deep inner soul... We're required to do these things just as salmon swim upstream.'

Neil Armstrong

The Apollo 11 astronauts, L-R: Neil A Armstrong, Michael Collins and Edwin E 'Buzz' Aldrin
Facing page: Buzz Aldrin on the surface of the moon. Notice the figure of Neil Armstrong and the lunar module reflected in the visor of Aldrin's space helmet

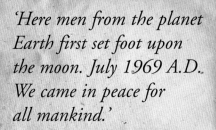

'Here men from the planet Earth first set foot upon the moon. July 1969 A.D. We came in peace for all mankind.'

Plaque left on the moon by the Apollo 11 astronauts

Imagine weightlessness!

Can you imagine what it would feel like to be weightless, like the astronauts on board Apollo 11? How would you cope with simple tasks such as getting dressed, washing your face or eating a bowl of cereal?

Write a short story about an imaginary day when your home or school was suddenly affected by 'zero gravity'.

Glossary

basaltic made from basalt, a type of volcanic rock

blubber whale fat, burned in lamps to give light

cannibal a person who eats the flesh of another person

cosmetics things that people put on their skin to improve the way they look

cosmonaut the word for a **Soviet** or Russian spaceman or woman

floes sheets of floating sea ice

horizon the line at which the earth and the sky appear to meet

International Date Line imaginary north-south line through the Pacific Ocean where the date changes by a day

landfall when you arrive on land after a sea or air journey

lunar to do with the moon

malaria a disease carried by mosquitoes which causes periods of fever in humans

malnutrition illness caused by not having the right food, or enough food, to eat

marooned left on your own in a remote place with little hope of escape

memento an object that reminds you of something or someone

missionary a person who goes to another country to spread a religious faith

mutiny a rebellion against authority, especially by soldiers and sailors against their leaders

orbit circular path of a spacecraft or other object around a star or planet

porters people who carry other people's baggage and possessions

putrid decaying, rotting or smelly

rapids in a river, where the water suddenly flows faster over rocks

rations when food is scarce and people are only allowed so much, to make it last as long as possible

salvage to save something, such as a ship's cargo, so that it can be used again

satellite a spacecraft which **orbits** a planet and collects information to send back to Earth

shroud a covering placed over a dead body before it is buried

Soviet Union a group of Communist countries formerly ruled by Russia; the Soviet Union began to break apart in 1985 and finally collapsed in 1991

specimen part or all of an animal, plant or object which is studied by a scientist

strait a narrow passage of sea between two or more pieces of land

surf the line of foam caused by waves breaking on a shore or beach

trek to make a long or difficult journey, usually on foot or on horseback

typhoid a disease in humans which causes fever, caught by eating bad food or drinking dirty water

Index

Webfinder

Pytheas
http://www.win.tue.nl/~engels/discovery/pytheas.html

Magellan
http://www.nmm.ac.uk/server/show/conWebDoc.142

Livingstone
http://www.livingstoneonline.ucl.ac.uk/biog/dl/bio.html

Kingsley
http://www.spartacus.schoolnet.co.uk/Wkingsley.htm

Shackleton
http://www.nmm.ac.uk/server/show/conWebDoc.189

Apollo 11
http://www.nasa.gov/centers/glenn/about/bios/neilabio.html